STARRY SKIES

Questions, Facts, & Riddles About the Universe

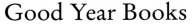

by Mike Artell

Good Year Books

*An Imprint of Addison-Wesley
Educational Publishers, Inc.*

WHOOSH!

Good Year Books

are available for most basic curriculum subjects plus many enrichment areas. For more Good Year Books, contact your local bookseller or educational dealer. For a complete catalog with information about other Good Year Books, please write:

Good Year Books
1900 East Lake Avenue
Glenview, IL 60025

Book design by Christine Ronan.
Copyright © 1997 Mike Artell.
All Rights Reserved.
Printed in the United States of America.

0-673-36350-3

5 6 7 8 9 -CRK- 05 04 03 02 01 00 99

Acknowledgement

My thanks to Matthew Dempsey, whose ideas for a book on astronomy for kids led to the book you now hold in your hands.

Photo Acknowledgments

Unless otherwise acknowledged, all photographs are the property of Addison-Wesley Educational Publishers, Inc. Abbreviations are as follows: (T) top, (B) bottom, (L) left, (R) right, (C) center, (BCKGRND) background.
• Front Cover, Back Cover, 4-5, 6-7, 11(B), 14-15, 19(B), 38-39, 40-41(B), 42-43, 44-45(B), 46-47(B), 48-49(B), 49(BR), 50-51(B), 52-53(B), 54-55(B), 56-57(B), 58-59(B), 60-61(B), 72-73, 79(B), 86-87 (BCKGRND), 88-89 (BCKGRND), 90-91 (BCKGRND), 92-93 (BCKGRND), 94-95 (BCKGRND), 96 (BCKGRND): National Optical Astronomy Observatories • Front Cover(T), 12(T), 19(T), 27(T), 30(T), 47(T), 49(C), 51(C), 56(T), 57(T), 59(C), 71(C), 77: Kitt Peak National Observatory/ National Optical Astronomy Observatories • Front Cover (B), 8-9, 10, 17 Hubble Space Telescope, 30(C), 30(B), 34-35, 37(T), 42(T), 45(T), 50(T), 54(T), 55(C), 56(T), 68, 70, 71(B), 74, 87(TL), 87(BL), 89(TL), 89(BL), 89(BR), 91(T), 95(T): NASA • 11(C): SOVFOTO/ EASFOTO • 13, 31: San Diego State University • 19(C): Kent Wood Photo Researchers, Inc. • 23: Fred Espenak/Science Photo Library/Photo Researchers, Inc. • 25(TL): David F. Malin/Anglo-Australian Telescope Board • 25(TR): Palomar Observatory • 25(BL): California Institute of Technology • 25(BR): © ROE/Anglo-Australian Telescope Board • 32(L), 32(R): San Diego University Library, Special Collections • 33: David F. Malin, © Anglo-Australian Telescope Board • 41(C), 48, 49(T) 52, 58(T), 87(TR), 87(BR), 93(R): JPL/NASA • 44-45: Rod Planck/Dembinsky Photo Associates • 47(C): Joe Sohm/Photo Researchers, Inc. • 75: © Meteor Crater Enterprise • 78: Giraudon/Art Resource • 79(T): Vivian Hoette, Adler Planetarium, Chicago, IL.

Do you know   W H E R E

You are in space on a giant ball of rock and water streaking around a huge mass of superheated gas on the edge of an immense galaxy. Amazing!

For thousands of years, human beings have gazed into the night sky and studied the objects in space, hoping to better understand their universe. This book will share some of what scientists have learned over the centuries about how the objects in space were formed, what they're made of, and their effects on each other.

But more than that, this book will give you a small glimpse of the awesome nature of the universe. It is a universe made up of an uncountable number of immense objects separated by incredible distances, all moving in a timeless dance. And you are part of it.

you are in the UNIVERSE?

This space trip isn't just about numbers and facts, though. Along the way, you'll find jokes, riddles, tongue twisters, and plenty of goofy characters who will help make your journey lots of fun.

So lock on to the nearest star and let's

O
F
F
!

L
I
F
T

Mike Artell has written and illustrated lots of books for children, several of which have received awards from major educational publications.

Mike didn't start drawing cartoons seriously until he was 27 years old, and he was 42 before his first book was published. But even though he started late, Mike caught up fast. This is his twenty-first book, not counting the twenty-four activity and coloring books he's done.

Each year, on average, Mike visits 50–60 schools, addresses six major educational conferences, conducts six writing/drawing workshops, and writes and illustrates three books. Then he rests.

Mike is married to Susan. They have two daughters, Stephanie and Joanna, who they suspect are from another planet.

All of the Artells currently live on Earth.

Table of CONTENTS

THE

WHOOSH!

SKY

What is THE SKY?

Think of the sky this way: As soon as you leave the surface of the Earth, you begin to enter the sky.

space

atmosphere

Earth

We call the part of the sky close to the Earth the **atmosphere.** Among other things, the atmosphere contains the air we breathe, dust particles, water molecules, and clouds.

When you leave the Earth's atmosphere, you enter the part of the sky we call **space**.

LOOK! I'M IN THE SKY!

We call it space because there's a lot of space between things out there. But that doesn't mean that space is empty. There are billions and billions of things floating around.

SATELLITES

On October 4, 1957, the Soviet Union launched *Sputnik 1*, the first man-made satellite placed in orbit around Earth. It fell to Earth after about three months and signalled the start of the "space race" between the United States and the Soviet Union.

SPACE JUNK

There are more than 50,000 pieces of "space junk" orbiting the Earth. "Space junk" includes small bits of metal, large pieces of rockets, and other stuff that hasn't fallen to Earth yet. This material could do a lot of damage to a satellite or the space shuttle if they collided.

Ding!

Bonk!

Chicken Little thought the sky was falling on her head. But I'll bet it was SPACE JUNK she really felt instead.

FOCUS ON FACTS

THE SPACE SHUTTLE

The Space Shuttle is an amazing vehicle. It's a laboratory for scientific experiments, a delivery truck for satellites, and a commuter bus for astronauts traveling to and from the Mir space station.

In addition to helping to launch satellites, the space shuttle also catches them. In the past when a satellite had a problem, scientists on the ground would try to "work around" the problem by sending a new set of commands to it. This would work sometimes, but many times the problem couldn't be fixed from the ground.

The space shuttle has helped to solve some of those problems. By using its robotic arm, the shuttle can catch a satellite and bring it close to the payload bay so that astronaut "mechanics" can fix it.

After the Hubble Space Telescope was in place, scientists discovered a flaw in one of the lenses. So they sent the space shuttle to the rescue! Astronauts flew the shuttle into space, made the necessary repairs, and placed the telescope back in its proper orbit.

Several years later, astronauts "caught" the Hubble Space Telescope again. During this mission, the astronauts did some maintenance work and replaced ten instruments to make the telescope even more powerful.

So you see, the space shuttle is not only a delivery truck, it's a pickup truck too!

What's out IN SPACE?

PLANETS   STARS

SPACE STUFF

COMETS

Whew! It would take a while to answer that question. That's because there's so much out there. There are stars and planets and comets and asteroids and meteors and moons and even some satellites we Earth people sent out into space. At this very moment there may even be a few astronauts in space.

And there are probably many, many more things out in space that we don't even know about yet.

THE

STARS

What is a STAR?

A **star** is a large object in space that is so hot, it glows. As the Sun glows or shines, its heat and light is radiated out into space. Being on the Sun is like standing near a glowing log in a fireplace.

Why are stars HOT?

Stars are formed when gases and dust in space get squeezed together by gravity. All this squeezing and pulling causes the gas and dust molecules to rub together and heat up.

A STAR IS BORN

GOO

Eventually, this hot ball of gas and dust becomes a giant nuclear power plant. The material in the star becomes so hot that it becomes pure energy. Some of the energy can be seen as light and some can be felt as heat. It is this energy that lights the Earth during the day and warms our atmosphere.

A new star goes through many changes, which eventually cause it to expand and then shrink. Over time, so much energy can build up inside the star that it explodes. What's left after the explosion is a different kind of star.

We call our star the Sun, but there are more stars in the universe than we can count.

Imagine you're flying through space and you see this weird-looking shape. What would you think it is?

It's an image taken by the Hubble Space Telescope of a huge column of gas and dust floating in space. Because the gases and dust are affected by gravity, radiation, and other factors, there's a good chance that new stars will develop here.

Diagram of a star

STAR FACT

All stars are not at the same temperature. The hottest stars are
- blue stars (20,000 to 45,000°F)

Next-hottest are
- blue-white stars (14,500 to 20,000°F)
- white stars (11,000 to 14,500°F)
- yellow-white stars (9,000 to 11,000°F)
- orange stars (6,500 to 9,000°F) and finally,
- red stars (5,500 to 6,500°F).

Our sun is a yellow-white star.

Our star THE SUN

The bad news is that our Sun is going to burn out. The good news is that it'll probably take about five billion years to do that.

If you compared our Sun to the other stars in the universe, it would look pretty average: not very big; not very small.

The surface of the Sun is very hot: almost 11,000°F. But that's nothing compared to the temperature at the center, or core, of the Sun, where the temperature rises to a blistering 27,000,000°F.

Scientists have seen some amazing sights while studying the Sun. One example is sunspots, which are actually areas of strong magnetic activity on the Sun's surface. Sunspots are darker and not quite as hot as surrounding areas. Sunspots come and go in cycles that last about 11 years. Some of the most dramatic sights are solar prominences and flares. Prominences can take different shapes, but they are often seen as huge loops or arches of hot gases given off by the sun. Flares are like solar storms that shoot bright bursts of energy away from the sun. These flares often give off energy that interferes with radio signals on Earth.

You can't see sunspots, prominences, or flares without using special equipment, so don't even try. You can damage your eyes permanently if you look directly at the Sun.

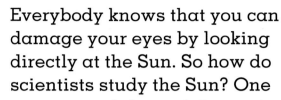

FOCUS ON *FACTS*

SOLAR TELESCOPE

The McMath-Pierce Solar Telescope at Kitt Peak National Observatory

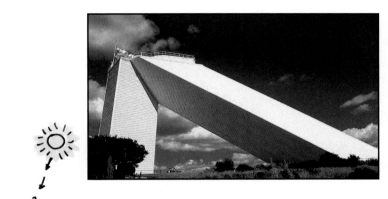

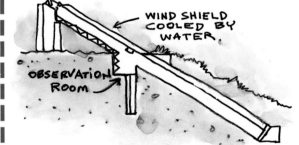

WIND SHIELD COOLED BY WATER.

OBSERVATION ROOM

Everybody knows that you can damage your eyes by looking directly at the Sun. So how do scientists study the Sun? One tool they might use is the solar telescope at Kitt Peak. This telescope focuses sunlight down an underground tunnel. The sunlight then passes through many filters. The resulting image is then safe for scientists to study closely. At Kitt Peak, they also have a vacuum tower solar telescope that has been used to keep records of solar magnetic activity for many years.

NEVER LOOK AT THE SUN!

Be safe. Watch a solar eclipse this way: Punch a hole in a piece of paper, then place another piece of paper under it.

SUNLIGHT

A little "movie" of the eclipse will appear on the bottom piece of paper.

The name for our star is the Sun.
To us, our Sun's number one.
Were it farther away, we'd be freezing today.
Were it closer, we'd all be well done.

Some stars are **binary** stars. To understand binary stars, you have to understand what the word **gravity** means.

GRAVITY

GRAVITY IS THE FORCE IN THE UNIVERSE THAT PULLS THINGS TOWARD EACH OTHER. IF YOU DROP AN OBJECT, THE FORCE THAT PULLS IT TOWARD THE GROUND IS GRAVITY.

GRAVITY→ ←BALL GROUND↓

GRAVY
BROWN, RED OR WHITE GOOPY STUFF THAT YOU POUR ON TOP OF POTATOES.

GRIN
TO SHOW YOUR TEETH WHEN YOU LAUGH. LIKE THIS→

Each binary star is actually two stars. Because they are so close together, the gravity field of each star pulls them together and causes them to spin around a central point in space. It almost makes them look as if they're dancing.

You may have heard about a kind of star called a **supernova.**

A supernova is an exploding star. When a supernova occurs, the outer layers of the star are blown away from the center, giving off tremendous amounts of energy. At the same time the center of the star shrinks down to a size smaller than it was before the explosion. Sometimes what's left of the star becomes a neutron star and begins to rotate rapidly. This spinning neutron star is called a **pulsar.**

What is a GALAXY?

A galaxy is a huge grouping of stars.

Because of the great distances between objects in space, it's hard for us to see the "big picture." But if you could get way, way out in space, you'd see that most of the stars in the universe are clustered together in groups. We call these groups of stars **galaxies.**

The MILKY WAY Galaxy

What is the name of OUR GALAXY?

We call our galaxy **the Milky Way.** Here's why: At night, we can see stars in the sky. Some of them are bright, but most are so faint that all we can see is a milky-looking cloud of light in the distance.

The ancient Greek astronomers saw this same milky cloud in the night sky.

Looks like milk to me.

FAST FACT

Our galaxy, the Milky Way, has about 100 billion stars.

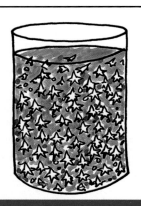

Since the Greek word for milk is *gala*, you can see how we got the word *galaxy* for a large group of stars. In keeping with this idea, we call the galaxy we're part of "the Milky Way." It's not the biggest galaxy in the universe, but it's still pretty big. If you could travel as fast as a beam of light (186,000 miles per second) it would take you 100,000 years to cross the Milky Way.

Scientists think that smaller galaxies may have fewer than a million stars and larger galaxies may have more than a trillion stars.

Galaxies come in a variety of shapes and sizes.

Spiral galaxies like the Milky Way are shaped like a disk and look like a pinwheel of stars.

Barred spiral galaxies have "arms" of stars that poke out of the center from which more stars swirl into a pinwheel shape.

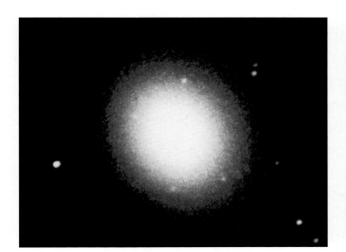

Elliptical galaxies can be almost oval-shaped or spherical like a globe.

Irregular galaxies are, well, irregular. They don't have any particular shape.

Scientists estimate that there are tens of billions of galaxies in the universe, and many of those galaxies each have billions of stars.

Is there LIFE on other planets?

The quick answer is, "We don't know. But we're trying hard to find out."

WHAT'S THE SLOW ANSWER?

Over the past few decades, we humans have sent landers and orbiters to other planets, and we've set up huge antennae hoping to hear radio signals from civilizations on other planets. Unfortunately, we've had no indication that there's anybody else out there. On the other hand, some scientists believe that there are just too many stars and planets in space for us to be the only ones around.

A scientist by the name of F. D. Drake developed a method for estimating the number of civilizations with whom we could communicate in our galaxy, the Milky Way. This method is called **the Drake equation.** When using the Drake equation, scientists estimate the number of stars in our galaxy, the fraction of those stars that are like our Sun, the average number of planets around those stars, the fraction of those planets that are suitable for life as we know it, and a number of other factors. The results vary, depending on the estimates the scientists use.

But the Drake equation is not proof of any other life in space. For now, we'll just have to keep looking and listening.

O.K... SO iF THERE ARE A BAZILLION STARS iN THE GALAXY AND A JILLION ARE LIKE THE SUN...

1,000,000,000

$E = MC^2$

$\sqrt{x \cdot \infty}$

$\propto \sqrt{z}$

FOCUS ON FACTS

RADIO TELESCOPES

The Radio Telescope at Arecibo, Puerto Rico

How do you get information about objects in space when the dust and gas in Earth's atmosphere make it difficult to see? Simple. Use a radio telescope. Instead of detecting visible light, radio telescopes detect the radio signals produced by objects in space.

Radio telescopes have been in use since the 1930s, but the largest one in use today is the telescope at Arecibo, Puerto Rico. It's about 1,000 feet in diameter and it fills up a whole valley.

Even though the reflecting dish looks like one smooth piece of metal, it is actually made up of more than 38,000 aluminum panels. Each panel has holes in it to allow rainwater to drain out.

Above the reflector is a gigantic triangle-shaped platform weighing about 600 tons. The platform is held in place by heavy cables attached to three huge concrete towers. The panels on the reflector below focus the radio signals captured from space onto antennae that are attached to the underside of the platform. The signals are then amplified. That means that they are made stronger. It's like turning up the volume on a stereo. Scientists can then study those signals.

Scientists in Arecibo are always updating and improving the telescope equipment so they can learn even more about this "invisible" kind of astronomy.

Will we ever TRAVEL to

Probably, although it will be a long time before we will send anyone outside our solar system.

Here's why: Imagine scientists wanted to send a group of astronauts to the planet Mars. Because Mars and Earth both orbit the Sun, the task of landing a spacecraft on Mars would be similar to riding on a merry-go-round and trying to throw a ball to someone in a car driving on a racetrack built around the merry-go-round.

If you wanted the person in the car to catch the ball, you would have to throw the ball at exactly the right moment, right? Furthermore, because of the effects of gravity, imagine you have to throw a perfect curve ball. To make things even harder, imagine that there's a lot of room between the merry-go-round and the racetrack and you're throwing a tiny little pebble instead of a ball. Seems almost impossible, doesn't it? Compared to a trip to Mars, this problem seems simple.

other planets?

Traveling at about 25,000 miles per hour, it would take months and months to reach Mars. It might even take a year. Why? Because both planets are moving in different orbits around the Sun and the spacecraft would have to travel in a huge curved arc. During the long trip, the astronauts would need food, water, rest, exercise, and entertainment. That would require a very large spacecraft with several crew members.

And guess what? After the space travelers reached Mars, it might take another whole year before Earth was in the right position for the return trip.

Then, once again, it could take as long as a year to return home.

Total time: three years. And that's for a planet that is relatively close to us. To reach the nearest star, Alpha Centauri, it would take four years just to get there, even if you traveled at the speed of light!

DAYS IN SPACE

For the time being, it looks as if the only places we'll be visiting are places in our solar system. But that's okay because there are plenty of things out there to see and learn about.

THE MIR SPACE STATION

The Mir Space Station

Often, scientists from two or more countries work together to learn more about space or share information they have gathered about the stars and planets. From time to time, they may even share a space station! The three people in this photograph are working together aboard the Russian space station Mir. From left to right, they are American astronaut Shannon W. Lucid, a guest researcher; cosmonaut Yuriy V. Usachov, flight engineer; and Commander Yuri I. Onufriyendo. Although Mir is permanently staffed by two or three people, visiting crews of up to six people have lived and worked on the space station for up to a month.

The Mir space station is actually made up of a number of pieces or modules. The first piece of the space station, called the core module, was launched on February 20, 1986. Over time, a number of different modules have been added. They include the astrophysics module known as the Kvant-1 and the scientific and airlock module known as the Kvant-2.

What is a CONSTELLATION?

Many years ago, as people looked at the night sky, they played "connect the dots" with the stars. They imagined pictures of animals and people in the sky and gave those pictures names. Those groups of stars with names are what we call **constellations.**

More on CONSTELLATIONS

In ancient times astronomers named constellations after people and animals like Gemini and Leo. In the 1500s and 1600s astronomers began traveling to South America and saw new constellations. They gave some animal names, such as the Fly, but they also named constellations after scientific equipment like the Microscope.

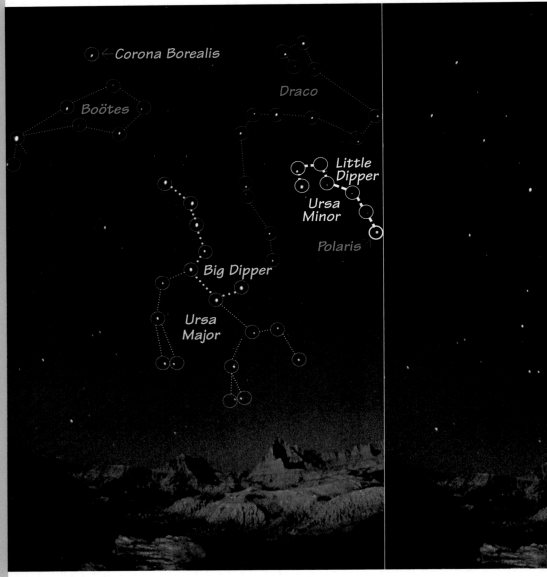

If you pointed a camera at the sky on a clear night and left the lens open, you would get a picture of the stars' "light trails" as the Earth turned.

If you stood in the right spot (called a celestial pole) and held the camera open long enough, the picture might look like the one on page 33.

The PLANETS in Our SOLAR SYSTEM

What is a PLANET?

A **planet** is a big, round ball of gas or rock that travels around a star. Some planets are also made up of ice or gases that are so cold they become liquids. The path a planet takes around a star is called the planet's **orbit.**

WANNA RACE?

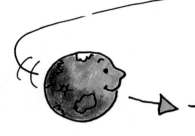

STAR

ORBIT

FOCUS ON FACTS

SIR ISAAC NEWTON

It's hard to talk about gravity, the planets, and telescopes without saying a few words about Sir Isaac Newton. Born in 1643, he may have been the greatest scientist of all time.

He built the first reflecting telescope, he was an expert in optics (a branch of science dealing with light and vision), and he laid the foundation for a kind of math called calculus. He may be best known, however, for his work involving gravity. An old story says Newton got his basic ideas about gravity by watching an apple fall from a tree. That may or may not be true, but everyone agrees that Sir Isaac Newton's ideas about the movement of objects in space have helped scientists make major advances in the science of physics.

Sir Isaac Newton died on March 31, 1727.

BOINK

When we say a planet is a BIG round ball, we mean BIG. The Earth is a planet and it is almost 8,000 miles across at its equator. As big as that is, some planets are much, much bigger.

COPERNICUS 1473–1543

Polish astronomer Nicolaus Copernicus is considered to be the founder of modern astronomy. He is best known for his theory that the Sun, not the Earth, is the center of our solar system. This seems pretty obvious to us today, but it got Copernicus into a lot of trouble. Why? Because hundreds of years earlier, another scientist named Ptolemy had said the Earth was the center of the solar system, and most people in power believed it. Fortunately, shortly before his death, Copernicus published his theory.

How do planets get ready for their orbits around a star?

They planet. (Plan it)

How many PLANETS are there

Pluto

I WONDER IF THERE'S ANY INTELLIGENT LIFE AROUND HERE...

Uranus

In our solar system, we know of nine planets. Their names are Mercury, Venus, Earth, Mars, Jupiter, Saturn, Uranus, Neptune, and Pluto.

One of the amazing things about our solar system is the way everything is in constant motion. The moons constantly revolve around the planets. The planets rotate and constantly revolve around the Sun. There are asteroids, comets, and meteors zooming around the solar system all the time, and the entire solar system is constantly in motion as it rides along on one of the spiral arms of our galaxy.

The Sun

Our Solar System

38 Mercury   Venus   Earth   Mars   Jupiter

in our solar system?

Are there other stars with planets?

There may be. Scientists have noticed changes in the movements of some nearby stars.

These changes in movement could mean that there are very large planets in the part of space near those stars.

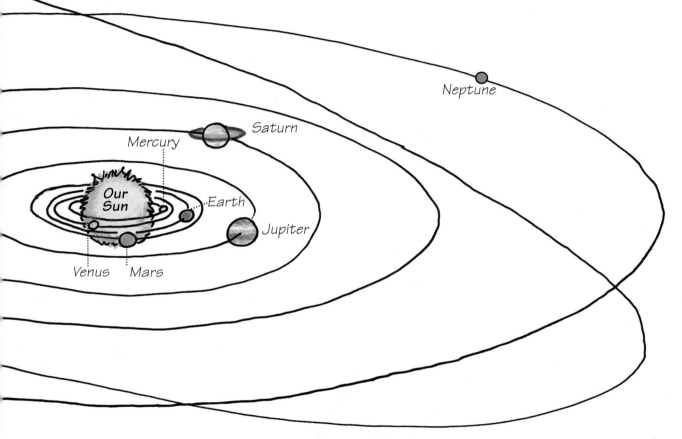

Are all planets in our solar system alike?

Nope. In fact, they're very different from each other. Some are made of rock and ice, and some are made of gases. Read on for a description of each one.

MERCURY

Mercury is closest to the Sun. It's about 36 million miles away. That may seem like a lot of miles, but the Sun is so big that any planet traveling that close to the Sun is going to be very, very hot. And Mercury is definitely hot! Scientists think that the side of Mercury facing the Sun has temperatures as high as 800°F.

Sometimes Mercury is so close to the Sun that from its surface the Sun would look about four times bigger in the sky than it does to us on Earth. No matter how much sunscreen you put on, it wouldn't help you on Mercury.

Mercury is also very small. It's only about 3,000 miles across at the equator. That's less than half the size of Earth. Because Mercury is so small and so close to the Sun, you usually can't see it in the sky. Don't even try! You can really hurt your eyes by looking at the Sun.

FAST FACT

The ancient Romans named Mercury after the mythological messenger of the gods.

MARINER 10 VISITS MERCURY

Mariner 10 was launched on November 3, 1973, and provided scientists with lots of new information about the planets Venus and Mercury. In fact, *Mariner 10* was the first spacecraft designed to study more than one planet. This image of Mercury was pieced together from many smaller photos taken by *Mariner 10*. The black shape at the bottom is a section of Mercury that

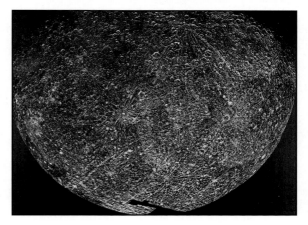

was not photographed. Notice all the craters on the surface. Looks a lot like our Moon, doesn't it?

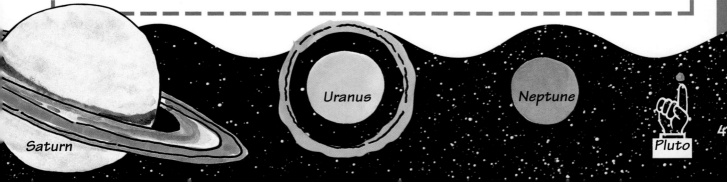

Saturn

Uranus

Neptune

Pluto

41

VENUS

PEE-YEW! I DON'T SMELL VERY GOOD.

The next planet is Venus. Venus is a little smaller than the Earth. It's about 7,500 miles across at its equator.

If you think Mercury is hot, you ought to check out this place. Even though it's farther away from the Sun, it's hotter than Mercury!

Why? Because Venus is covered with a layer of clouds made up mostly of sulfuric acid.

Much of the heat from the Sun that reaches Venus gets trapped beneath these clouds and can't get out. It's like being inside a giant greenhouse that stays hot. Really hot. Incredibly hot! It gets so hot that even some metals would melt on the surface of Venus.

ER.... BAD NEWS HOUSTON. MY SHIP MELTED.

A DAY ON VENUS

When is a day longer than a year?
When it's on Venus!

A *day* is the amount of time it takes a planet to rotate once on its axis. A *year* is the amount of time it takes a planet to orbit the Sun.

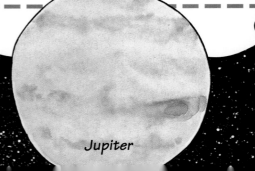

Another weird thing about Venus is that it rotates in the opposite direction from Earth and most of the other planets. Most of the planets rotate from west to east, or counterclockwise. Venus rotates east to west, or clockwise.

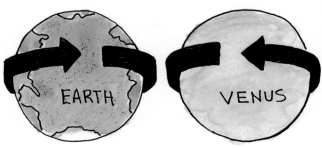

Venus is approximately 67,200,000 miles from the Sun. Even though Venus and Earth are similar in size, density, and distance from the Sun, they are different in almost every other way.

I LIKE BEING DIFFERENT!

I DON'T LIKE BEING RUSHED.

Because Venus rotates on its axis very, very slowly, it takes about 243 Earth days for it to make one rotation.

Meanwhile, Venus is zooming around the Sun on an orbit that takes about 225 Earth days to complete. The result? On Venus, a day is actually longer than a year!

Saturn

Uranus

Neptune

Pluto

EARTH

Good old planet Earth is the third planet from the Sun. It takes the Earth 365 days to travel around the Sun. We call this a **year.** At a certain time during this year, the northern half of Earth is tilted a little more toward the sun. This is what we call **summer.** During the winter, the northern half of Earth is tilted away from the Sun.

Even though most of the Earth is covered with water, the center of the Earth is red hot. In fact, the core of Earth is made up of melted metals more than 7,000°F. Sometimes that heat works its way through all the layers of rocks and minerals and escapes to the surface.

SUN

Earth is a great place to live if you like to breathe. In fact, it's the only place in our solar system with the right atmosphere for life as we know it.

Two gases make up most of the Earth's atmosphere: nitrogen (76%) and oxygen (21%). These gases, along with small amounts of many other gases, make up the air we need to breathe.

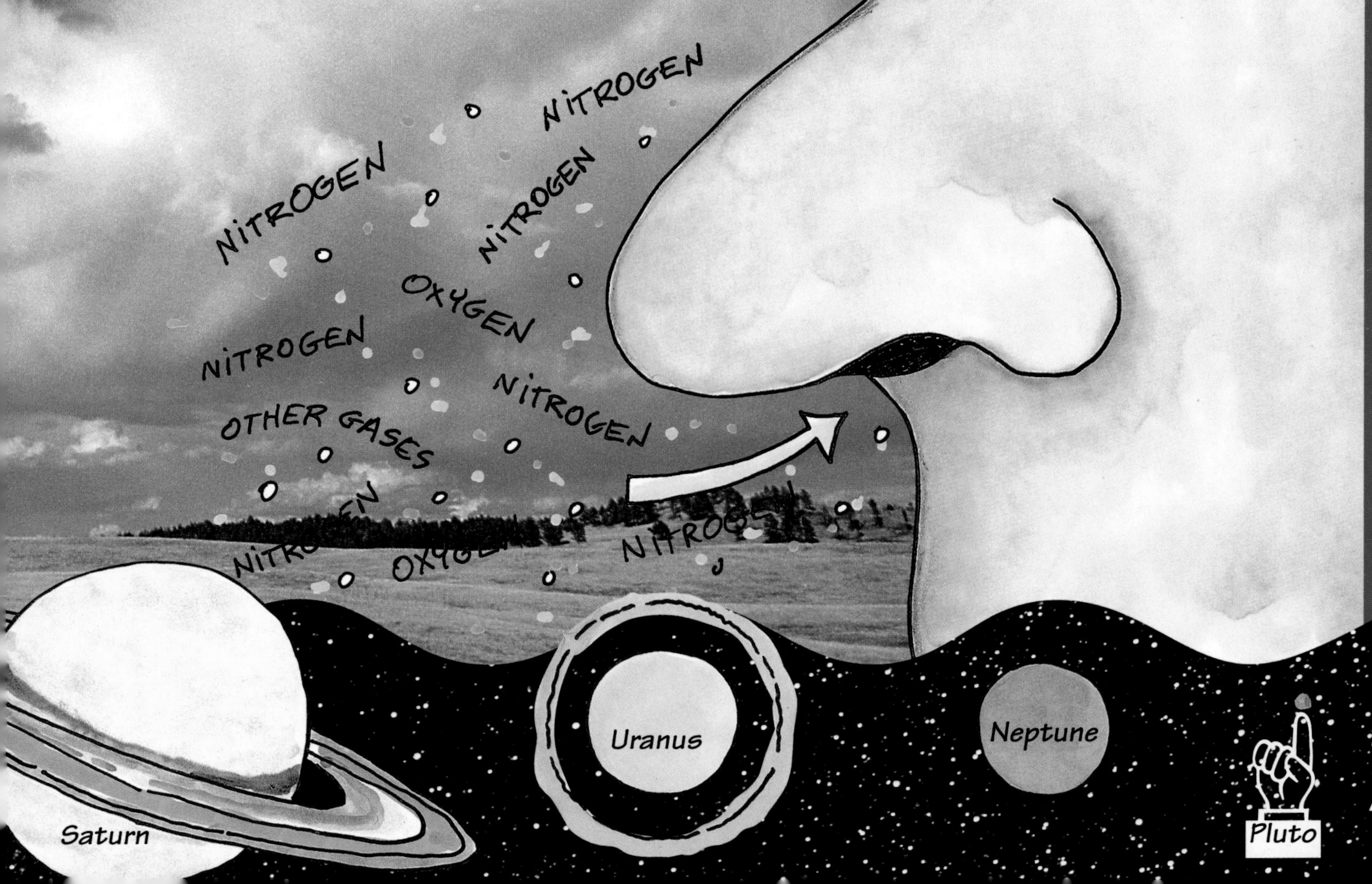

NITROGEN
NITROGEN
NITROGEN
NITROGEN
NITROGEN
OXYGEN
NITROGEN
NITROGEN
OTHER GASES
NITROGEN
NITROGEN
OXYGEN
NITROGEN

Saturn

Uranus

Neptune

Pluto

45

More about EARTH

Earth is the only planet that we know has liquid water on its surface.

This comes in handy for creatures like us, whose bodies are about 90% water. It means we have plenty of water to drink and enough moisture in our atmosphere.

Earth is about 7,900 miles across at its equator and is approximately 93,000,000 miles from the Sun. That seems to be the perfect distance for people, animals, and plants on Earth to survive.

FAST FACT

Yoo-Hoo! I'M UNDER ALL THESE CLOUDS!

Most of the time, about half of the Earth's surface is covered by clouds.

FOCUS ON FACTS

A VERY LARGE ARRAY

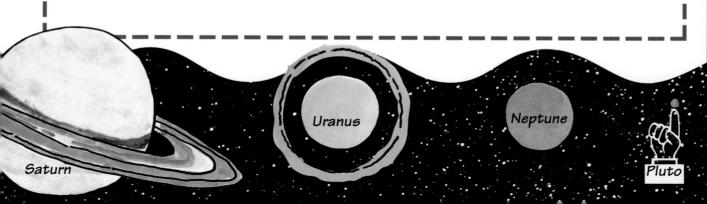

For many years, scientists wanted to find a way to get more and more optical and radio data from space, but the cost and difficulty of building bigger and bigger telescopes was always a problem.

One way scientists found they could work around this problem is by gathering data from arrays of telescopes. An array is a group of objects that have been set up in some special order or arrangement. By setting up many telescopes in an array and linking them together electronically, scientists can take samples of images and data received by each telescope and combine all of the information. The results are almost like using a single telescope that is as large as the distance between each telescope.

In New Mexico, there is a Very Large Array (VLA) that has 27 telescopes spread over 24 miles. Each telescope is more than 80 feet in diameter and weighs approximately 200 tons. The telescopes can be moved on railroad tracks that are laid in a giant Y shape so scientists can arrange them for each observation.

Saturn

Uranus

Neptune

Pluto

MARS

Mars is 4,200 miles across, about half the size of Earth. It's a great planet to watch through a telescope because it doesn't have much of an atmosphere. That means you can look right at the surface of the planet, just as you can look at our Moon.

Mars is approximately 142,000,000 miles from the Sun, but sometimes Mars gets very close to the Earth, which makes it even easier to see.

A long time ago, Mars had active volcanoes. They seem to have quieted down, but before they stopped, they created the largest volcano in our solar system. It's called Olympus Mons and it's more than 17 miles high. Just to give you an idea of how tall that is, the tallest mountain on Earth is Mount Everest in Nepal. It's a little over five miles high. Olympus Mons is three times taller than Mount Everest!

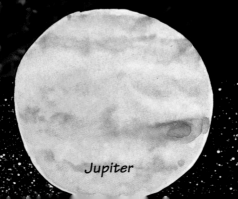 

Some scientists think that Mars may once have been more like Earth. It may have had liquid water, and that means it may have had some forms of life on it.

FOCUS ON FACTS

PATHFINDER ON MARS

On July 4, 1997, the *Pathfinder* spacecraft bounced onto the surface of Mars. Airbags surrounding *Pathfinder* cushioned its rough landing. Although the curved flight path taken by *Pathfinder* was more than 312,000,000 miles long, it landed within 30 miles of the exact target. Amazing!

After landing, *Pathfinder's* small robot rover "Sojourner" rolled across the surface of Mars and sampled the Martian dust and rocks. The information *Sojourner* gathered was then radioed back to scientists on Earth.

Scientists are already planning additional flights to Mars to learn even more about "the red planet."

TONGUE TWISTER
Many
Martians
Making
Marching
Motions

Saturn

Uranus

Neptune

Pluto

JUPITER

JUPITER
EARTH

Jupiter is the biggest planet in our solar system. Here's a quick size comparison: Earth is almost 8,000 miles across at its equator. Jupiter is more than 88,000 miles across at its equator. That's eleven times larger! In fact, Jupiter is actually bigger than all the other planets in our solar system combined.

It's also a long, long way from the Sun. While Earth is about 93,000,000 miles away from the Sun, Jupiter is more than 480,000,000 miles away. That's more than five times farther from the Sun.

Because Jupiter is so far away, it takes a long, long time for it to orbit the Sun. In fact, it takes almost twelve years for Jupiter to make a complete orbit.

The Sun

Our Solar System

Mercury

Venus

Earth

Mars

Jupiter

50

One of the first things you notice when you look at Jupiter is the Great Red Spot.

The Red Spot is actually a giant storm on the surface of Jupiter. Astronomers have been watching this storm for hundreds of years and it shows no signs of stopping.

By the way, you probably wouldn't want to try to land on Jupiter. There's no solid surface, the outer layers are really cold, while the inner layers are really hot, and you couldn't breathe. Besides that, it would take you years to get there.

OUCH! THIS THING REALLY ITCHES!

SCRATCH SCRATCH

FOCUS ON FACTS

JUPITER'S SWEET SIXTEEN

Scientists have discovered a total of 16 moons circling Jupiter, although some of the smaller ones may actually be asteroids.

Four of the larger moons (Io, Europa, Ganymede, and Callisto) were discovered by Galileo in the year 1610. With a telescope you can actually see these moons moving across the face of Jupiter, although Callisto is dark and can be hard to see.

Saturn

Uranus

Neptune

Pluto

SATURN

Saturn is the planet with all the beautiful rings around it. Actually, Jupiter, Uranus, and Neptune have rings too, but not as many and they are not as bright as Saturn's. Saturn is a huge planet and, in our solar system, is second in size only to Jupiter. At the equator, it is about 75,000 miles across.

Saturn is far from the Sun. How far? 889,000,000 miles! The same rays from the Sun that take about 8 1/2 minutes to reach Earth would take about one hour and twenty minutes to get to Saturn.

Even though Saturn is huge, it's not very dense. In other words, it's like a giant gas marshmallow. If you could find a tub of water big enough to hold Saturn, it would actually float!

Our Solar System

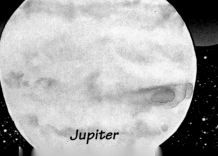

Mercury   *Venus*   *Earth*   *Mars*   *Jupiter*

In the year 1610, a scientist named Galileo saw Saturn through his telescope.

The telescope had only recently been invented, so as you might guess, the one Galileo used wasn't as good as the ones we have today. When he looked at Saturn, it looked a little blurry. He thought the rings were bumps on the sides of the planet. To him, it looked like a "triple" planet.

About 45 years later, another scientist named Huygens (using a better telescope) identified the bumps as a ring around the planet. As telescopes got better, scientists later discovered separate rings.

In 1980 and 1981, the *Voyager 1* and *Voyager 2* spacecrafts took close-up pictures of Saturn and discovered that the planet actually has tens of thousands of rings.

Saturn

Uranus

Neptune

Pluto

URANUS

Uranus is another big planet made up mostly of gas, but it's smaller than Jupiter and Saturn. It's approximately 31,600 miles across at its equator.

Uranus is a long, long way from the Sun. How far? Oh...about 1,790,000,000 miles. That's about twice as far from the Sun as Saturn and about nineteen times as far from the Sun as Earth.

But the really weird thing about Uranus is that it's lying on its side. That means its side is really its top. Sort of. Confused? Maybe this will help. The axis around which Uranus rotates is tilted 98 degrees.

HMM.... THINGS LOOK A LITTLE DIFFERENT FROM THIS ANGLE.

To understand what this means, picture yourself sitting on the ground with your legs crossed. If you tilted yourself 90 degrees, you'd be lying on your side. Uranus is tilted even a little more than this.

The top of your body would still be the top of your body, but it would be in a strange position. That's the way Uranus is "sitting" in space.

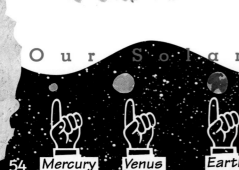

FOCUS ON FACTS

VOYAGER 1 & 2

In the late 1970s and early 1980s the orbits of the planets Jupiter, Saturn, Uranus, and Neptune were going to put them closer together than they usually are. So scientists developed the *Voyager 1* and *Voyager 2* spacecrafts to fly to that part of the solar system and gather data. The original plan was to study only Jupiter and its large moon Io and Saturn and its large moon Titan. But after studying these planets, scientists were able to reprogram the *Voyager* spacecrafts for a new mission.

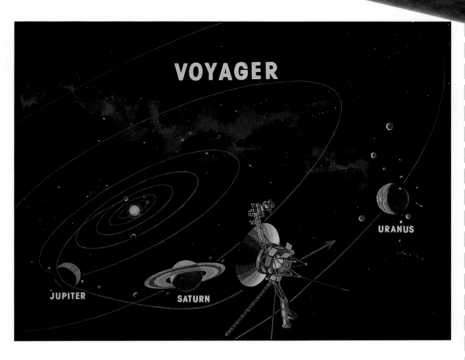

Voyager 1 was programmed to fly out of the solar system toward interstellar space. *Voyager 2* gathered data as it flew by Uranus and Neptune, and then it too was redirected toward interstellar space. By any measure, the *Voyager* missions were a huge success.

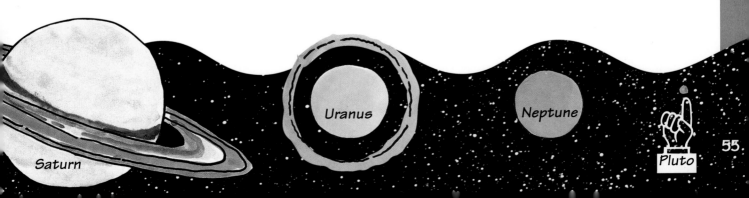

Saturn

Uranus

Neptune

Pluto

NEPTUNE

Go out another billion miles or so from Uranus and you'll find Neptune.

In case you weren't taking notes, that means that Neptune is approximately 2,800,000,000 miles from the Sun. It's similar in size to Uranus... about 30,800 miles at its equator. Also, like Uranus, it's made up mostly of gases.

BURP

OOPS... EXCUSE ME!

NAME THAT PLANET

WHAT KIND OF MUSIC DO PLANETS LIKE?

NEP-TUNES

FAST FACT

Neptune was named for the Roman god of the sea.

FOCUS ON FACTS

GALILEO GALILEI

One of the greatest scientists of all time was Galileo Galilei. He was born in Italy in the year 1564 and studied both mathematics and medicine. In 1609 Galileo heard about a new invention called the **telescope.** He soon began building his own telescopes and used them to make observations of the Moon, planets, and stars.

LOOK OUT BELOW!

In addition to his work as an astronomer, Galileo also became noted in other areas of science. He invented the thermometer, created his own pendulum clock, and was especially interested in studying falling objects. In one of his most famous experiments, Galileo dropped two steel balls, one large and one smaller, from a tall tower to prove his theories about gravity. Which ball do you think hit the ground first? Neither! They both hit the ground at the same time, just as Galileo had predicted.

Saturn

Uranus

Neptune

Pluto

PLUTO

Pluto was discovered in 1930. It's amazing that scientists even found Pluto floating in space because it's such a tiny planet and so far away. Pluto is the smallest and usually the most distant planet in our solar system.

It takes Pluto 248 years to orbit the Sun, and for about 20 of those years, Pluto is actually closer to the Sun than Neptune. That's because Pluto's orbit is more oval than circular. The diagram to the right will give you an idea of how it looks.

Even though Pluto is a very tiny planet, it has a moon, which is named Charon. Charon is only about 600 miles across at its equator. You can see it in the fuzzy photograph above.

And how big is Pluto? Look at a map of the United States. At its equator, Pluto is about as big as the distance between Houston, Texas, and Las Vegas, Nevada. That's about 1,400 miles—not very big compared to the other planets in our solar system.

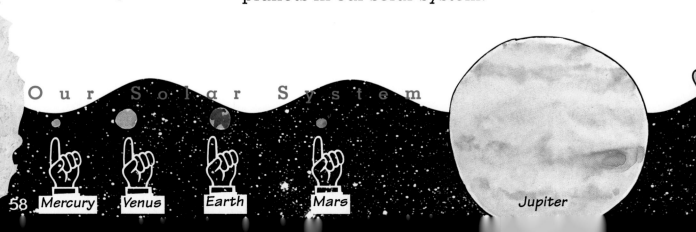

Our Solar System

Mercury   Venus   Earth   Mars   Jupiter

Pluto is approximately 3,670,000,000 miles from the Sun. To use our sunlight example again, it would take rays from the Sun traveling at 186,000 miles per second about 5 1/2 hours to reach Pluto.

Because of Pluto's great distance from Earth, it's a little difficult for scientists to study the planet closely. Currently, scientists believe that Pluto is made up of about 80% rock and 20% ice. Also, Pluto is lying on its side almost as much as Uranus is.

FOCUS ON FACTS

SOME TROUBLE WITH HUBBLE

On April 24, 1990, NASA launched the Hubble Space Telescope. Scientists would now be able to view distant objects without the effects of the Earth's atmosphere.

But there was bad news. One of the edges on the Hubble's main mirror was not perfectly smooth and the images from Hubble were fuzzy. There were also problems with the solar panels on Hubble.

On December 2, 1993, a team of astronauts flew the shuttle orbiter *Endeavour* on a Hubble repair mission. They installed some small mirrors to solve the "fuzzy vision" problem.

Today, the Hubble telescope can see just fine and is providing scientists with incredible images of distant objects in space.

Saturn

Uranus

Neptune

Pluto

Remembering the planets' NAMES

GREAT IDEA! Here's a way to remember the names of the planets in order:

Just remember this sentence: **"My Very Excited Mother Just Served Us New Pizza."**

The first letter of each word in that sentence is the first letter of the names of each of the planets. And they're in the right order!

My	**M**ercury
Very	**V**enus
Excited	**E**arth
Mother	**M**ars
Just	**J**upiter
Served	**S**aturn
Us	**U**ranus
New	**N**eptune
Pizza	**P**luto

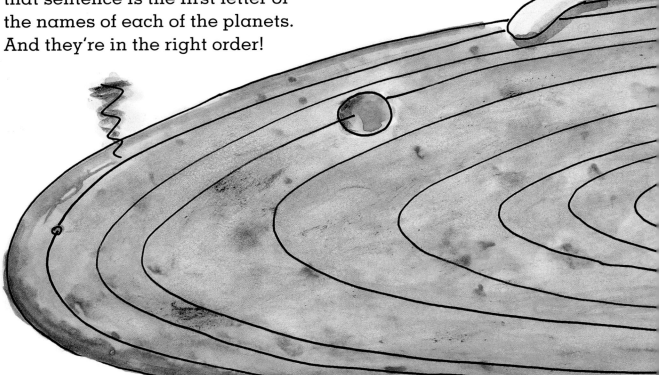

Mercury   Venus   Earth   Mars

Jupiter

Saturn

Uranus

Neptune

Pluto

You

YOU are HERE in

You and about 5,000,000,000 other people are on the planet Earth.

Earth is one of nine known planets that circle the Sun.

The Sun is one of billions of other stars in the Milky Way galaxy.

THE UNIVERSE

Does the universe sound crowded? It's not. Even with all the dust, gas, comets, meteoroids, asteroids, moons, planets, and stars, most of the universe is made up of empty space between objects.

There are billions of galaxies clustered throughout the universe.

Shrinking our SOLAR SYSTEM

Imagine we could shrink the Sun until it was about the same height as a professional basketball player. If the Sun was a little over 7 feet tall, here's what would happen to the rest of the solar system:

Sun diameter = 7-foot basketball player

Mercury = pea, ½ mile from the Sun

Venus = penny, 1 mile from the Sun

Earth = penny, 1½ miles from the Sun

Mars = aspirin, 2¼ miles from the Sun

Mercury would be about the size of a pea and would be more than ½ mile from the Sun.

Earth and Venus are about the same size. After we shrank the solar system, both planets would be a little larger than a penny. Venus would be more than a mile from the Sun, and Earth would be almost 1½ miles from the Sun.

Mars would be about as big across as an aspirin tablet and would be almost 2¼ miles from the Sun.

W A Y Down to Size!

Uranus and Neptune are about the same size. In our shrunken solar system example, they would both be about the size of a hard ball. And talk about a long way off! Uranus would be more than 28 miles from the Sun and Neptune would be about 44 miles from the Sun.

Jupiter = soccer ball, 7 1/2 miles from the Sun

Saturn = cabbage, 14 miles from the Sun

Uranus = hard ball, 28 miles from the Sun

Neptune = hard ball, 44 miles from the Sun

Pluto = tick, 58 miles from the Sun

Jupiter is the biggest planet, but in this example, it would shrink down to about the size of a soccer ball. And Jupiter would be more than 7 1/4 miles from the Sun.

Saturn would be about the size of a small cabbage and would be just about 14 miles from the Sun.

Pluto may be the most amazing example of all. If the sun was about the size of a professional basketball player, Pluto would be about the size of a tick and it would be a whopping 58 miles from the Sun!

How Did Our SOLAR SYSTEM

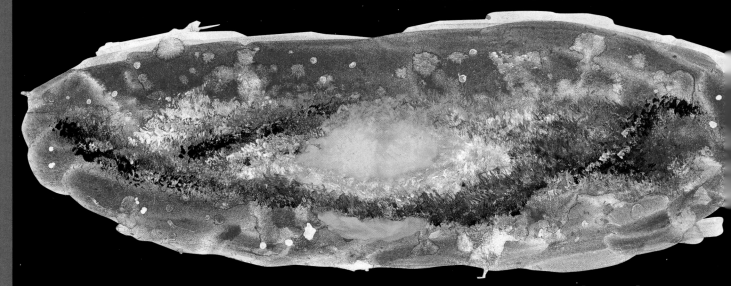

Nobody was around with a video camera, so it's hard to know. But scientists think they have a pretty good idea. Most of them believe that our part of the universe started out filled with a huge cloud of gas and dust. For some reason, a long, long time ago, that cloud began to shrink and get more dense. As the cloud shrank, the energy that drew the particles of dust and gas together was converted into heat. This is how our Sun was formed.

O.K. THIS IS GOING TO BE ON THE TEST, CLASS... THE IMPORTANT THING TO REMEMBER ABOUT OUR SOLAR SYSTEM IS THAT EVERYTHING IN IT REVOLVES AROUND THE SUN. GOT IT?

PLANETS

SUN

Get Started?

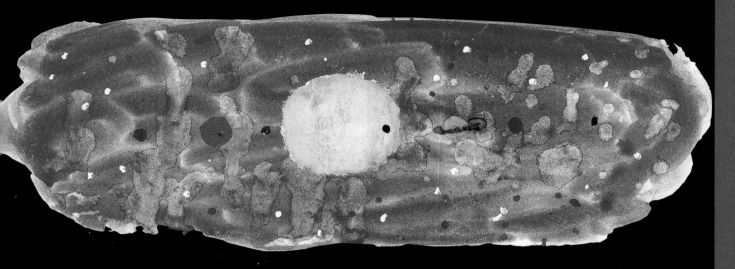

Scientists believe that the whole time this collapse was taking place, the cloud of gas and dust was spinning. It spun slowly at first, then faster as the collapse took place. With the new Sun as the center, the larger pieces of spinning rock and dust attracted smaller pieces and, over time, asteroids, moons, and planets formed. This spinning motion continues as the orbits of the objects in our solar system.

DUCK EVERYBODY! HERE THEY COME AGAIN!

What's the difference between a PLANET and a MOON?

The PLANET Jupiter

MOONS of Jupiter

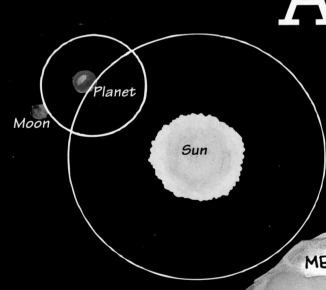

Moon

Planet

Sun

A planet revolves around a star. A moon revolves around a planet. And moons are usually smaller than planets.

Do all the planets in our solar system have moons?
No, but most of them do. Mercury and Venus are the only planets in our solar system without moons.

MERCURY

VENUS

WAAAHH... EVERYBODY ELSE HAS MOONS AND WE DON'T HAVE ANY...

And how many moons
do the other planets have?
They'll tell you.

Earth's MOON

The moon is our nearest neighbor in space. It's only about 230,000 miles away, which is pretty close in space distances.

approximately
← 2,160 →
miles

THE MOON

Every 27.3 days, the Moon circles Earth. The Moon also spins on its own axis at the same rate, so we earthlings always see the same side of the Moon. We can see the Moon so well because sunlight bounces off the surface of the Moon and makes it shine. Because the Moon and Earth are constantly revolving and moving through space, we sometimes see the moon as a big, round circle, and then later see it as a tiny crescent-shaped slice. We call these different shapes the **phases of the Moon.**

Ancient Romans believed moonlight could affect their brains. Their word for moon was luna and that's where we get our word lunatic.

Many scientists believe the Moon was formed when a huge object in space collided with Earth and giant chunks of rock were thrown out into space. The Moon also has lots of craters showing where objects have struck its surface. In 1969, scientists got a chance to study the moon up close as astronaut Neil Armstrong became the first person to set foot on the Moon. Armstrong and other Moon-visiting astronauts have brought back many samples of dust and rocks from the Moon for scientists to study.

Phases of the Moon

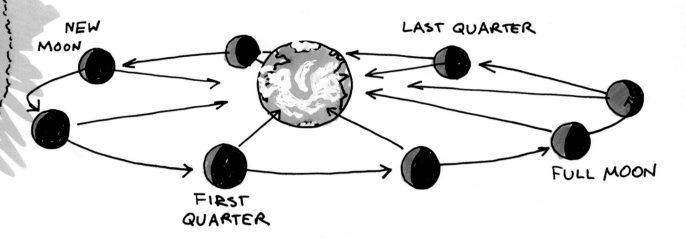

NEW MOON

LAST QUARTER

FIRST QUARTER

FULL MOON

FOCUS ON FACTS

APOLLO 11

On July 20, 1969, astronauts Neil Armstrong and Edwin (Buzz) Aldrin, Jr., became the first human beings to land a spacecraft on the Moon. They landed their craft, nicknamed *Eagle*, on the area of the Moon called Mare Tranquillitatis, which means Sea of Tranquility.

The astronauts walked on the Moon (Armstrong was the first person to walk on the Moon!), collected rock samples to bring back to Earth, took many photographs, and set up some scientific experiments. The astronauts had to wear bulky space suits, like the one shown in this picture, to provide them with oxygen, to protect them from the harsh temperatures on the Moon, and to allow them to communicate.

ASTEROIDS, METEOROIDS, and COMETS

What is an ASTEROID?

You can think of asteroids as really big rocks or really small planets.

The largest asteroid is named Ceres. It's about 600 miles across. While that's a pretty big rock, it's still less than half the size of Pluto, the smallest planet. Most asteroids are nowhere near this big. Scientists think that most of them are probably one mile or less in diameter.

I'M SO CONFUSED... AM I A ROCK OR A PLANET?

ASTEROID:

MARS

O.K. YOU ASTEROIDS, BREAK IT UP!

If you were going on an asteroid hunt, you'd find most of the asteroids in our solar system between Mars and Jupiter. Scientists think that lots of asteroids are there because Jupiter's strong forces kept those asteroids from joining together to form a planet-sized object.

What is a METEOR?

What most people call a meteor is really a meteoroid.

The small asteroids that are on a collision course with Earth but have not yet entered Earth's atmosphere are called **meteoroids**. Often, when meteoroids enter Earth's atmosphere, friction makes them and the air molecules around them heat up until they produce flashes of light. These flashes of light are called **meteors**. Most meteoroids burn up as they enter Earth's atmosphere, but some survive the trip and strike Earth. The meteoroids that strike the surface of Earth are called **meteorites**.

This is Barringer Meteorite Crater in Arizona. It was formed when a meteorite hit Earth many years ago. The crater is 4,150 feet across and 570 feet deep.

Meteors have another name too. They're sometimes called shooting stars or falling stars.

Tongue Twister:
Shooting stars should start shooting shortly.

What is a METEOR SHOWER?

A meteor shower has nothing to do with soap and water. We see a meteor shower when lots of meteoroids burn up in our atmosphere at once. The greatest meteor shower on record occurred on the evening of November 16 and early morning of November 17, 1966.

REMEMBER THIS... A METEOR IS NOT SOMETHING YOU COULD HOLD. A METEOR IS A FLASH OF LIGHT.

WHAT KIND OF SHOWERS DO LITTLE ASTEROIDS TAKE?

METEOR SHOWERS!

What is a COMET?

A comet is a dirty iceball.

It's true. A comet is a ball of ice and dust particles and some gases. As a comet moves closer to the Sun, these materials heat up and are pushed away by radiation and energy particles emitted by the Sun.

That's what gives a comet its "tail." Actually *tail* isn't a very accurate term, because the tail is always pushed away from the Sun. This means the tail sometimes points in an odd direction. In fact, if a comet is moving away from the Sun, its tail will actually be ahead of it.

A DIRTY ICEBALL? I'VE NEVER BEEN SO INSULTED!

A comet's tail gets longer as it gets closer to the sun →

SUN

Famous COMETS

ISTIMIRANT STEIIA

This piece of cloth was made in the year 1066. It shows astronomers pointing at Halley's Comet!

One of the most famous comets is Halley's comet. Do you know anyone born in 1986? That was the last time Halley's comet visited our part of the solar system.

This comet is named for the English astronomer Edmond Halley. In 1682 Halley saw a comet through his telescope and was able to calculate its orbit. He realized that this was probably the same comet that was seen in the year 1531 and again in 1607. That meant that the comet reappeared about every 76 years. Halley then predicted that the comet would return in the year 1758. And guess what? It did! Unfortunately, Halley died in 1742, so he wasn't around to see it.

The last time Halley's comet came close to Earth was in the year 1986. Since scientists knew it was on the way (thanks to Halley), they were able to send spacecraft near the comet to study it.

Comet watchers have had several chances over the past few years to see comets in the night sky. In March 1993, the comet Kohoutek passed about 370 million miles from the Sun and was just barely visible from Earth.

In March 1997, the comet Hale-Bopp passed about 120 million miles from Earth. That's it in the photo to the right. It was clearly visible to the naked eye. If you missed it, sorry. You'll have to wait about 2,380 years for it to come around again.

The Halley's Comet Rap

Instructions: Slowly and rhythmically stamp your feet twice and clap once. Then, recite this rap:

Halley saw a comet back in 1682.
He did some calculations, and
    then when he was through,
He said, "This comet needs a
    name, I'm sure you will agree,
And if you don't object, I think I'll
    name it after ME!"

Astronomers all know that
    Halley's comet still appears,
But please don't hold your breath,
    the trip takes seventy-six years.
We saw it last in nineteen eighty six, that's
    what I'm told,
And next time Halley's comet comes around
    I'll sure be old!

WOKKA WOKKA

BLACK HOLES

and Other Stuff

What is a BLACK HOLE?

Imagine a "hole" in the sky with gravity so strong that even rays of light get pulled back into the hole before they are radiated into space. That's what scientists think a black hole is like.

Black holes are so tightly packed that their gravitational pull is many, many times stronger than anything on Earth. Because black holes have a huge gravitational pull for their size, not even light is fast enough or strong enough to escape. And get this: scientists think time may actually slow down in and around a black hole. That's how powerful its gravity is.

Black holes have something in common with the wind. Even though we can't see the wind, we can see its effects. Trees sway in the breeze, sailboats get pushed along, and clouds slowly float through the sky. Like the wind, black holes are invisible, but scientists can see the effects that black holes have on the space around them.

HMMM... I DON'T SEEM TO BE AGING QUITE AS FAST AS BEFORE.

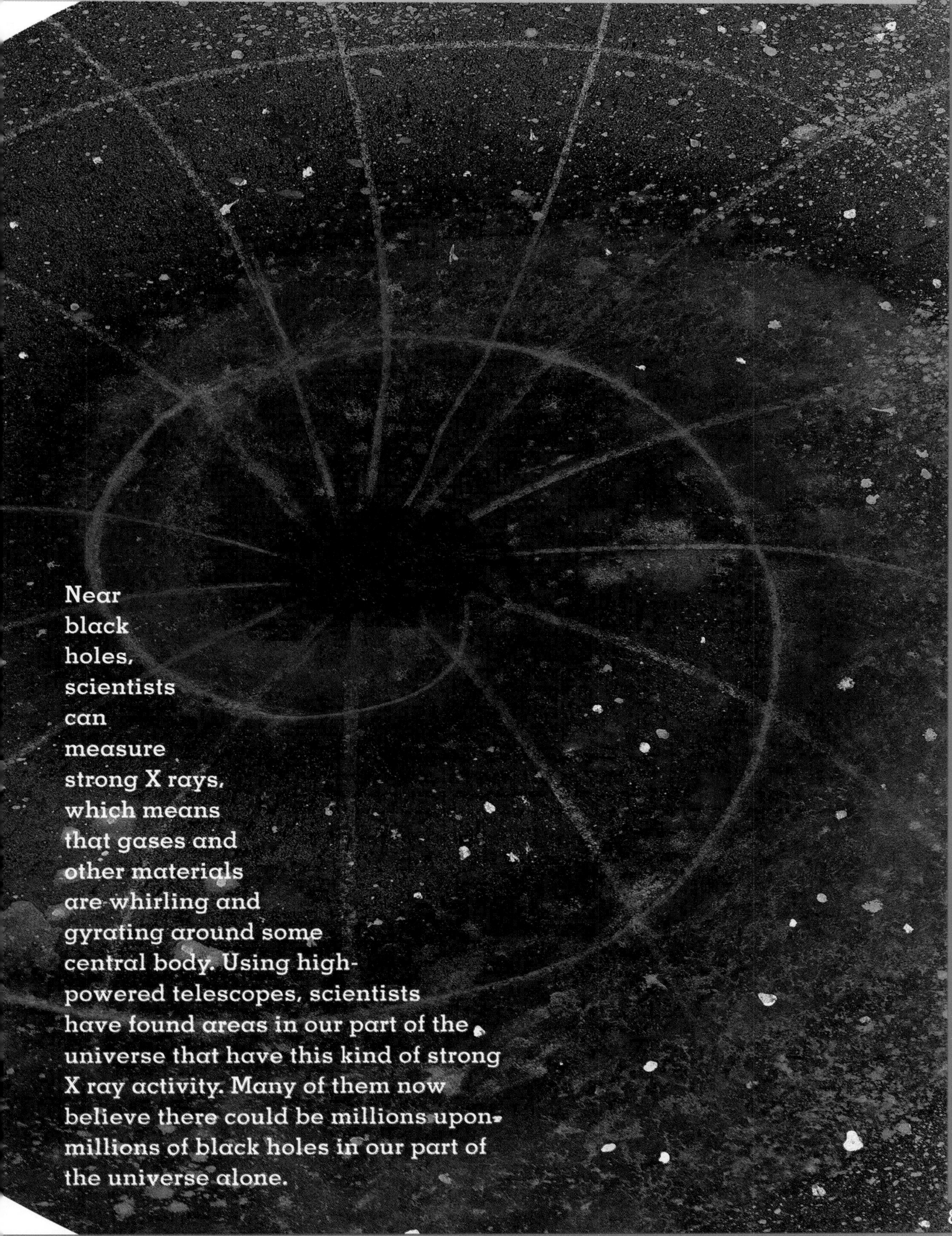

Near
black
holes,
scientists
can
measure
strong X rays,
which means
that gases and
other materials
are whirling and
gyrating around some
central body. Using high-
powered telescopes, scientists
have found areas in our part of the
universe that have this kind of strong
X ray activity. Many of them now
believe there could be millions upon
millions of black holes in our part of
the universe alone.

What causes BLACK HOLES?

YOUR BASIC AVERAGE STAR...

GETS BIGGER AND HOTTER...

SUPER NOVA

UNTIL...

KA-BLOOEY IT EXPLODES!

WHAT'S LEFT BEGINS TO SHRINK

AND FORMS...

TA DAH! A BLACK HOLE!

As stars become supernovas and explode, what remains begins to shrink. Stars that were very dense and tightly packed can shrink so much and become so dense that they become black holes.

BLACK HOLE BRAIN BUSTERS

ANSWERS ARE AT THE BOTTOM OF PAGE 86

CAN YOU MAKE AT LEAST 15 WORDS FROM THE LETTERS IN THE WORDS, "BLACK HOLE?"

WHAT'S THE DIFFERENCE BETWEEN A BLACK HOLE IN OUTER SPACE AND A HURRICANE IN A DISTANT PLACE?

What is a LIGHT YEAR?

POP ↓

POP QUIZ

QUESTION: WHAT IS A LIGHT YEAR?

① A YEAR WHEN YOU LOSE A LOT OF WEIGHT.

② HOW LONG A LIGHT BULB LASTS BEFORE IT BURNS OUT.

③ THE NUMBER OF MILES A BEAM OF LIGHT TRAVELS IN A YEAR.

THE CORRECT ANSWER IS NUMBER 3!

If a beam of light can travel 186,000 miles in just one second, think how far it can travel in a whole year! To find out how far this is, you'd have to figure out how many seconds are in a year, then multiply that times 186,000.

So, what's the answer? To find out, turn the book upside down.

FAST FACT

The closest star to the Sun (Alpha Centauri) is about four light years away. That means that the light we see from that star actually left the star four years ago! The light we see from some stars left hundreds or even thousands of years ago!

In a year, a beam of light can travel approximately 5,880,000,000,000 miles. That's 5 trillion, 880 billion miles!

How to Make Your SPACE MOBILE

Here's a space mobile that you can make. You'll need a pair of scissors, tape, two coat hangers, string or thread, some twist ties, and a push pin. First, place one coat hanger onto the other so it forms an X shape. Wrap the twist ties around the spots where the coat hangers touch to hold them together.

Next, with a pair of scissors, cut out each of the objects (planets, comet, etc.) on the following pages. If you like, you can laminate each of the objects to make them stronger. Tape the objects to pieces of string. Cut some of the strings long and some short. One at a time, tie the other end

of each string to the coat hangers.

Continue hanging objects from the coat hangers at different points to balance your mobile. Finally, stick a push pin into

the ceiling of your room. Tie one end of a piece of string to the hooks of the coat hangers and the other end around the push pin.

Tah Dah! You did it!

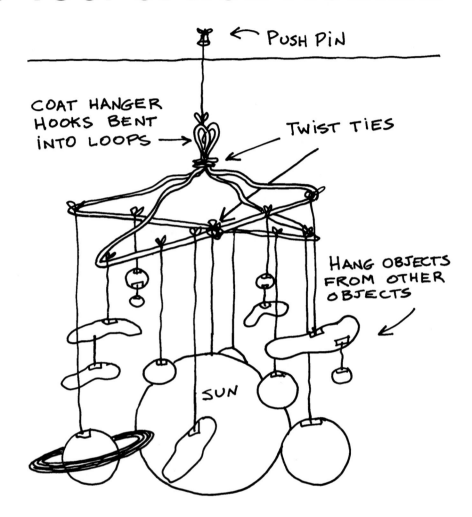

PUSH PIN

COAT HANGER HOOKS BENT INTO LOOPS →

TWIST TIES

HANG OBJECTS FROM OTHER OBJECTS

SUN

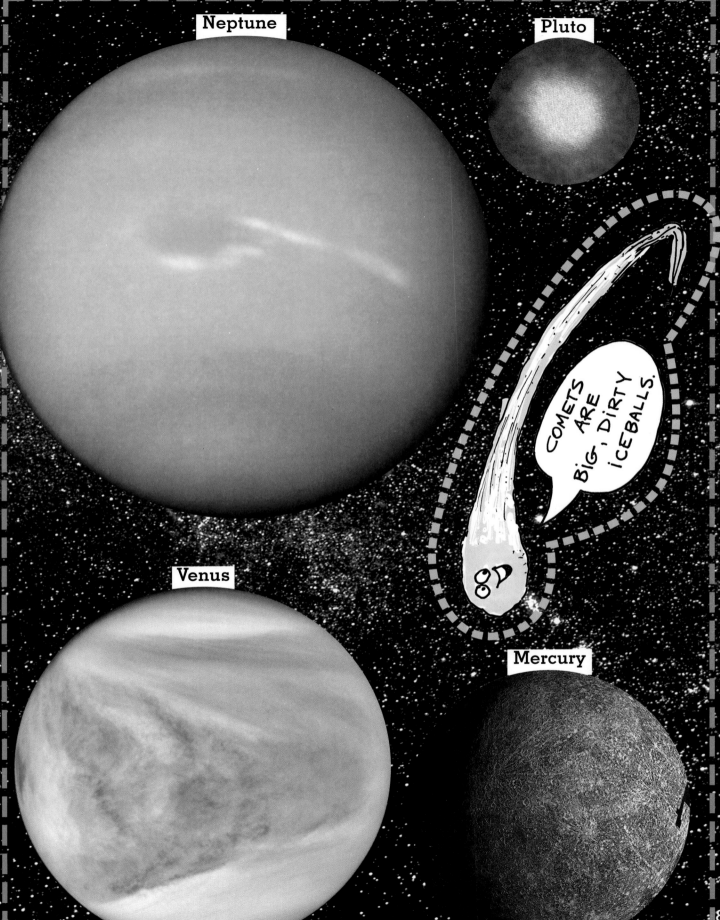

Uranus

Earth

Mars

Jupiter
NEXT TO THE SUN, I'M THE BIGGEST GUY IN THE SOLAR SYSTEM.
HUBBLE
SPACE TELESCOPE
WOW! WHAT A VIEW!

Saturn